JR. GRAPHIC AMERICAN INVENTORS

STEVE JOBS

Jane Gould

PowerKiDS press™

New York

Published in 2013 by The Rosen Publishing Group, Inc.
29 East 21st Street, New York, NY 10010

First Edition

Editor: Joanne Randolph

Book Design: Planman Technologies

Illustrations: Planman Technologies

Library of Congress Cataloging-in-Publication Data

Gould, Jane.

Steve Jobs / by Jane Gould. — 1st ed.

　　p. cm. — (Jr. graphic American inventors)

Includes index.

ISBN 978-1-4777-0080-8 (library binding) — ISBN 978-1-4777-0145-4 (pbk.) — ISBN 978-1-4777-0146-1 (6-pack)

1. Jobs, Steve, 1955–2011—Juvenile literature. 2. Computer engineers—United States—Biography—Juvenile literature. 3. Businessmen—United States—Biography—Juvenile literature. 4. Apple Computer, Inc.—History—Juvenile literature. I. Title.

QA76.2.A2G68 2013

338.7'6100416092—dc23

[B]

2012020633

Manufactured in the United States of America

CPSIA Compliance Information: Batch #W13PK1: For Further Information contact Rosen Publishing, New York, New York at 1-800-237-9932

Contents

Introduction

Steve Jobs was a man with a vision. He wanted to make computer **technology** easy for people to use. By doing that, he also changed the way people used technology. His company, Apple Inc., created **devices** like the iMac, the iPod, the iPhone, and the iPad. These inventions had a huge effect on computers, music, and phones. Steve Jobs will always be remembered for creating beautiful, useful, and exciting **products**. He led the way into a new age of technology.

Main Characters

Paul (1922–1993) and Clara Jobs (1924–1986) Steve's parents. They **adopted** him when he was a baby. Paul was a Coast Guard veteran and a machinist. Clara worked as a bookkeeper.

Steve Jobs (1955–2011) Businessman, **visionary**, and **entrepreneur** who started Apple Inc. It was one of the first companies to make **personal computers**.

Joanne Schieble (1932–) Jobs's **biological** mother. She gave him up for adoption.

John Scully (1939–) A businessman who ran Apple from 1983 until 1993.

Steve Wozniak (1950–) Jobs's friend and business partner. They started Apple Computers together. Wozniak created the Apple I and Apple II.

STEVE JOBS

STEVEN PAUL JOBS WAS BORN IN SAN FRANCISCO, CALIFORNIA, ON FEBRUARY 24, 1955. HE AND THE COMPANY HE COFOUNDED, APPLE INC., CREATED PRODUCTS THAT CHANGED THE WAY THE WORLD USES TECHNOLOGY.

JOBS'S BIOLOGICAL PARENTS MET AT THE UNIVERSITY OF WISCONSIN. HIS FATHER WAS ABDULFATTAH JANDALI, A SYRIAN. HIS MOTHER, JOANNE SCHIEBLE, WAS AMERICAN. THEY GAVE STEVE UP FOR ADOPTION.

I CANNOT MARRY YOU. MY PARENTS WILL NOT LET ME.

WE MUST DO WHAT IS BEST FOR THE BABY. I WANT HIM TO HAVE A GOOD LIFE.

CLARA AND PAUL JOBS ADOPTED STEVE. AT FIRST, SCHIEBLE WOULD NOT LET THEM TAKE HIM. SHE WANTED HER BABY'S PARENTS TO BE COLLEGE GRADUATES. THEY WERE NOT.

SHE WILL LET YOU ADOPT HIM ONLY IF YOU PROMISE TO SEND HIM TO COLLEGE.

WE WILL, EVEN IF IT TAKES EVERY CENT I EARN.

PAUL AND CLARA HAD NO CHILDREN BEFORE STEVE. THEY WERE HAPPY TO HAVE A CHILD AT LAST. THREE YEARS LATER, THEY ADOPTED ANOTHER CHILD, PATTY.

HE IS SO BEAUTIFUL! LET'S NAME HIM STEVEN PAUL.

THE JOBSES LIVED IN MOUNTAIN VIEW, CALIFORNIA, IN WHAT IS NOW CALLED SILICON VALLEY. STEVE AND HIS FATHER LIKED TO MAKE **ELECTRONIC** DEVICES IN THEIR GARAGE.

I GOT YOU THIS KIT.

WOW! I CAN BUILD MY OWN RADIO!

PAUL SHOWED STEVE HOW TO TAKE THINGS APART AND PUT THEM BACK TOGETHER. STEVE LEARNED HOW ELECTRONICS WORKED.

SEE, STEVE, YOU CAN BUILD THINGS THAT MIGHT SEEM IMPOSSIBLE AT FIRST.

STEVE WAS A VERY SMART CHILD, BUT HE DID NOT ALWAYS DO WELL IN SCHOOL. HIS FOURTH-GRADE TEACHER **BRIBED** HIM TO STUDY. HE ENDED UP DOING SO WELL THAT HE SKIPPED FIFTH GRADE.

IF YOU GET AN A ON YOUR MATH TEST, I'LL GIVE YOU ANOTHER CANDY BAR.

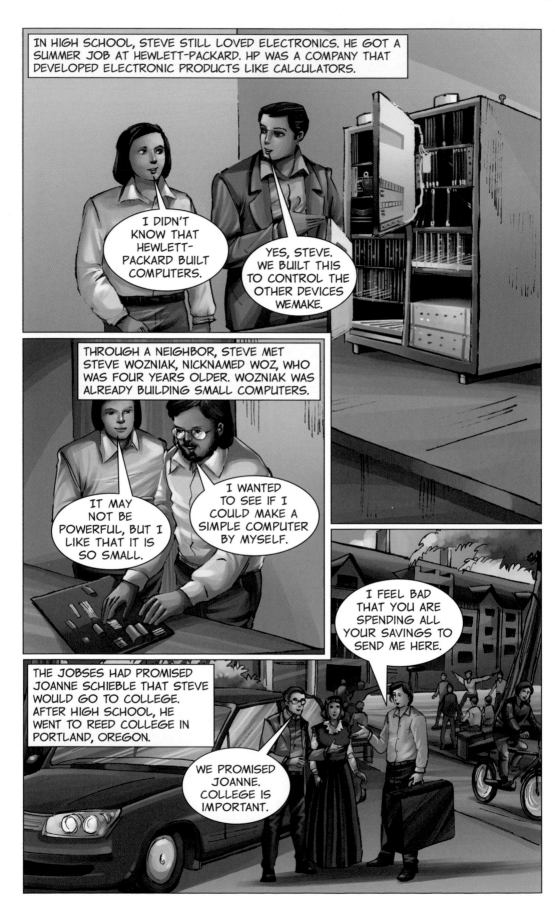

IN HIGH SCHOOL, STEVE STILL LOVED ELECTRONICS. HE GOT A SUMMER JOB AT HEWLETT-PACKARD. HP WAS A COMPANY THAT DEVELOPED ELECTRONIC PRODUCTS LIKE CALCULATORS.

I DIDN'T KNOW THAT HEWLETT-PACKARD BUILT COMPUTERS.

YES, STEVE. WE BUILT THIS TO CONTROL THE OTHER DEVICES WE MAKE.

THROUGH A NEIGHBOR, STEVE MET STEVE WOZNIAK, NICKNAMED WOZ, WHO WAS FOUR YEARS OLDER. WOZNIAK WAS ALREADY BUILDING SMALL COMPUTERS.

IT MAY NOT BE POWERFUL, BUT I LIKE THAT IT IS SO SMALL.

I WANTED TO SEE IF I COULD MAKE A SIMPLE COMPUTER BY MYSELF.

I FEEL BAD THAT YOU ARE SPENDING ALL YOUR SAVINGS TO SEND ME HERE.

THE JOBSES HAD PROMISED JOANNE SCHIEBLE THAT STEVE WOULD GO TO COLLEGE. AFTER HIGH SCHOOL, HE WENT TO REED COLLEGE IN PORTLAND, OREGON.

WE PROMISED JOANNE. COLLEGE IS IMPORTANT.

JOBS WAS NOT SURE WHAT HE WANTED TO DO WITH HIS LIFE. HE DROPPED OUT OF COLLEGE AFTER SIX MONTHS, BUT HE KEPT GOING TO CLASSES.

CAN YOU BELIEVE ALL THE DIFFERENT STYLES FOR LETTERS, STEVE?

I LOVE HOW SIMPLE AND BEAUTIFUL MANY DESIGNS ARE.

IN 1974, JOBS WENT TO WORK FOR ATARI, ONE OF THE FIRST VIDEO-GAME COMPANIES. JOBS WAS EXCITED THAT PEOPLE WANTED TO BUY ELECTRONIC GAMES.

THIS PONG GAME IS SELLING FASTER THAN PINBALL MACHINES.

I THINK PEOPLE WILL MAKE A LOT OF MONEY FROM COMPUTER GAMES.

AFTER A FEW MONTHS, JOBS LEFT ATARI AND WENT TO INDIA. HE WANTED TO THINK ABOUT WHAT TO DO WITH HIS LIFE. HE LEARNED ABOUT INDIAN RELIGIONS.

7

JOBS CAME BACK TO THE UNITED STATES AFTER SEVEN MONTHS. HE JOINED A COMPUTER CLUB WITH HIS FRIEND STEVE WOZNIAK.

CLUB MEMBERS MADE THEIR OWN SMALL PERSONAL COMPUTERS. BEFORE THEN, MOST COMPUTERS WERE VERY LARGE. ONLY BUSINESSES OR COLLEGES COULD AFFORD THEM.

WELCOME TO THE HOMEBREW COMPUTER CLUB.

DID THOSE GUYS MAKE THAT COMPUTER?

I MADE THIS ONE FROM A KIT.

WHAT DOES IT DO BESIDES BLINK ON AND OFF?

WOZNIAK SHOWED JOBS A COMPUTER HE HAD CREATED. IT WAS A **CIRCUIT BOARD** THAT COULD BE ATTACHED TO A KEYBOARD AND SCREEN. IT WAS MADE FOR PEOPLE TO USE IN THEIR OWN HOMES.

I MADE THIS FROM JUST A FEW PARTS. IT KEPT THE COST DOWN.

THIS WILL MAKE IT EASIER FOR ANYONE TO HAVE A COMPUTER.

PLUS, THEY WON'T HAVE TO FIGURE OUT WHERE ALL THE WIRES GO.

JOBS WANTED TO START MAKING COMPUTERS WITH WOZNIAK. THEY HOPED TO SELL THEM TO PEOPLE IN THE COMPUTER CLUB AND TO PEOPLE WHO DID NOT WANT TO MAKE THEIR OWN COMPUTERS.

WOZNIAK STARTED WORK ON A BETTER APPLE COMPUTER. THE APPLE II WAS READY IN 1977. IT HAD A PLASTIC CASE, A KEYBOARD, GOOD SOUND, COLOR **GRAPHICS**, AND THE APPLE LOGO.

OTHER COMPANIES MADE PERSONAL COMPUTERS. HOWEVER, WOZNIAK'S DESIGN MADE THE APPLE II SPECIAL. IT WAS EASY TO **PROGRAM**. USERS COULD ADD FEATURES AND **SOFTWARE**.

JOBS WENT TO ANOTHER COMPUTER FAIR TO SELL THE APPLE II. THIS TIME, HE GOT A LOT OF ATTENTION AND SOLD 300 COMPUTERS.

WE'RE GOING TO BE MILLIONAIRES!

THE APPLE II MADE MANY TYPES OF WORK FASTER AND EASIER. PEOPLE BEGAN TO FEEL THEY NEEDED A COMPUTER. AFTER ONLY FOUR YEARS, APPLE WAS A SUCCESSFUL COMPANY.

IN 1984, APPLE CREATED A NEW COMPUTER CALLED THE MACINTOSH. IT HAD A NEW FEATURE CALLED A MOUSE. PEOPLE USED THE MOUSE TO POINT AT PICTURES ON THE SCREEN AND CLICK ON THEM.

IT WILL MAKE USING A COMPUTER AS EASY AS USING A TOASTER.

BEFORE THE MACINTOSH, PEOPLE USED CODES AND TEXT TO RUN COMPUTERS.

IT LOOKS LIKE IBM COMPUTERS ARE SELLING VERY WELL.

YES, BUT OUR COMPUTERS ARE FOR YOUNG, CREATIVE PEOPLE.

AT FIRST, MANY PEOPLE WANTED TO BUY A MACINTOSH. HOWEVER, OTHER COMPANIES, LIKE IBM, ALSO MADE PERSONAL COMPUTERS.

THE MACINTOSH COULD NOT BEAT THE SALES OF IBM COMPUTERS. APPLE WAS LOSING MONEY.

THE MAC MAY COST MORE, BUT IT IS BETTER THAN AN IBM!

I AGREE, BUT THE IBM ALSO RUNS MORE SOFTWARE THAT PEOPLE WANT.

STEVE IS NOT SUPPORTING THE COMPANY AS HE SHOULD.

EVEN WOZNIAK IS THINKING OF LEAVING APPLE.

BY THIS TIME, APPLE HAD BECOME A VERY BIG COMPANY. JOBS DID NOT EVEN RUN IT ANYMORE. THE COMPANY PRESIDENT, JOHN SCULLY, THOUGHT THAT JOBS WAS CAUSING PROBLEMS.

DUE TO TENSIONS WITHIN THE COMPANY, JOBS LEFT APPLE. HE WAS ONLY 30 YEARS OLD. HE TOOK TIME OFF TO THINK ABOUT WHAT ELSE HE COULD DO.

I AM LEAVING APPLE FOR GOOD, BUT I WOULD STILL LIKE TO WORK WITH COMPUTERS.

IN 1985, JOBS DECIDED TO START HIS OWN COMPANY, CALLED NEXT. HE WANTED TO BUILD VERY POWERFUL COMPUTERS.

I'M EXCITED ABOUT MY NEW COMPANY, AND THE NEXT WORKSTATION IS INCREDIBLE.

JOBS ALSO BOUGHT A SMALL **ANIMATION** COMPANY, NOW KNOWN AS PIXAR. PIXAR USED COMPUTERS TO MAKE ANIMATED MOVIES. JOBS WANTED ITS NEW COMPUTER TECHNOLOGY.

AREN'T YOU IMPRESSED BY THE COMPUTER ANIMATION?

YOUR TECHNOLOGY IS AMAZING, BUT MOVIES DON'T INTEREST ME MUCH.

BY 1993, BOTH NEXT AND PIXAR WERE FAILING. JOBS PUT LOTS OF MONEY AND EFFORT INTO BOTH COMPANIES. IT DID NOT SEEM TO BE WORKING. JOBS'S LIFE REACHED A LOW POINT.

YOU ARE STILL LOSING A LOT OF MONEY.

I HAD TO SELL MOST OF NEXT. NOW I WILL TRY TO SELL PIXAR, TOO.

TOY STORY

I AM GOING TO MAKE BACK ALL THE MONEY THAT I LOST.

THINGS WERE ABOUT TO CHANGE, THOUGH. IN 1995, PIXAR'S MOVIE *TOY STORY* CAME OUT. THE MOVIE WAS A HUGE SUCCESS, AND LATER THAT YEAR, STEVE JOBS BECAME A BILLIONAIRE.

BY 1997, APPLE WAS LOSING LOTS OF MONEY. THE COMPANY ASKED JOBS TO COME BACK AND TAKE CONTROL. IT HAD BEEN 12 YEARS SINCE HE LEFT APPLE.

I WILL RUN APPLE ONLY UNTIL IT IS DOING WELL AGAIN. THEN, I'M LEAVING.

WHY WOULD SOMEONE BUY THAT MACHINE? IS IT REALLY USEFUL?

JOBS GOT TO WORK RIGHT AWAY. HE TALKED TO APPLE WORKERS TO SEE WHICH PRODUCTS WERE THE BEST. HE HAD THE COMPANY STOP MAKING DEVICES THAT WERE NOT MAKING MONEY.

JOBS DECIDED HE WANTED APPLE TO MAKE ONLY FOUR GREAT COMPUTERS. THEY WOULD BE A DESKTOP AND LAPTOP FOR HOME USERS AND A DESKTOP AND LAPTOP FOR **PROFESSIONAL** USERS.

CAN WE MAKE ENOUGH MONEY WITH SO FEW PRODUCTS?

IF OUR COMPUTERS STAND OUT, WE WILL.

IN UNDER A YEAR, JOBS INTRODUCED THE TWO NEW PROFESSIONAL COMPUTERS: THE POWER MAC AND POWERBOOK.

OUR FANS, AND EVEN THOSE WHO HAVEN'T USED A MAC, WILL SEE THAT OUR COMPUTERS STILL MEET THEIR NEEDS BETTER THAN ANY OTHER COMPUTER.

THE NEW COMPUTERS WERE A BIG HIT. APPLE STARTED MAKING MONEY AGAIN.

NOW THAT STEVE JOBS IS BACK, I BOUGHT A NEW MAC.

I DO ALL MY DESIGNING ON MACS.

IN 1998, JOBS INTRODUCED A NEW COMPUTER CALLED THE IMAC. IT WAS DESIGNED TO BE PART OF A **NETWORK**.

THE IMAC COULD CONNECT TO OTHER COMPUTERS. IT DID NOT HAVE TO CONTAIN ALL THE PARTS ITSELF.

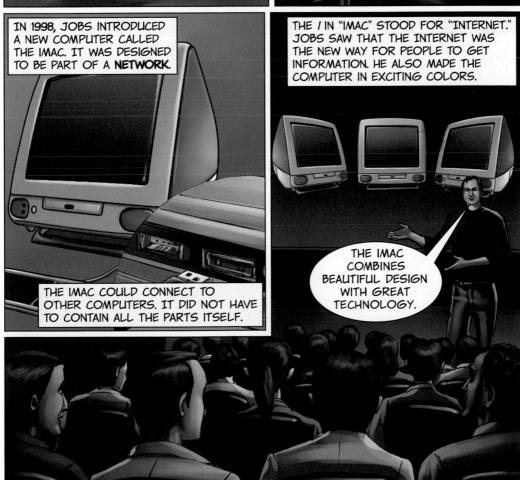

THE *I* IN "IMAC" STOOD FOR "INTERNET." JOBS SAW THAT THE INTERNET WAS THE NEW WAY FOR PEOPLE TO GET INFORMATION. HE ALSO MADE THE COMPUTER IN EXCITING COLORS.

THE IMAC COMBINES BEAUTIFUL DESIGN WITH GREAT TECHNOLOGY.

THE IMAC SOLD VERY WELL. THE NEXT YEAR, JOBS INTRODUCED THE COLORFUL IBOOK, THE LAPTOP VERSION OF THE IMAC.

JOBS HELPED APPLE BECOME SUCCESSFUL AGAIN. THREE YEARS AFTER HE RETURNED, HE DECIDED HE WOULD CONTINUE TO RUN THE COMPANY.

I SAID I WOULD STEP DOWN ONCE THE COMPANY WAS MAKING MONEY, BUT I STILL HAVE A LOT OF IDEAS.

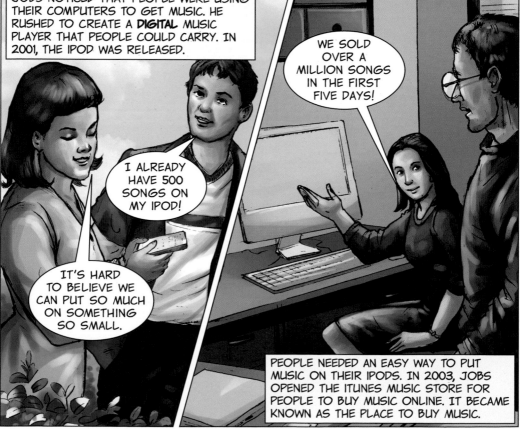

JOBS NOTICED THAT PEOPLE WERE USING THEIR COMPUTERS TO GET MUSIC. HE RUSHED TO CREATE A **DIGITAL** MUSIC PLAYER THAT PEOPLE COULD CARRY. IN 2001, THE IPOD WAS RELEASED.

I ALREADY HAVE 500 SONGS ON MY IPOD!

IT'S HARD TO BELIEVE WE CAN PUT SO MUCH ON SOMETHING SO SMALL.

WE SOLD OVER A MILLION SONGS IN THE FIRST FIVE DAYS!

PEOPLE NEEDED AN EASY WAY TO PUT MUSIC ON THEIR IPODS. IN 2003, JOBS OPENED THE ITUNES MUSIC STORE FOR PEOPLE TO BUY MUSIC ONLINE. IT BECAME KNOWN AS THE PLACE TO BUY MUSIC.

EVERYTHING SEEMED TO BE GOING RIGHT FOR JOBS. THEN, IN OCTOBER 2003, HIS DOCTORS FOUND THAT HE HAD CANCER. JOBS HAD SURGERY THE NEXT YEAR. HE TOLD EVERYONE THAT HE WAS CURED.

I CAN STILL RUN THE COMPANY. I WOULD STEP DOWN IF I COULDN'T.

TODAY APPLE IS GOING TO REINVENT THE PHONE.

APPLE CONTINUED TO GROW AND MAKE EXCITING NEW DEVICES BESIDES COMPUTERS. IN JANUARY 2007, JOBS ANNOUNCED A NEW PRODUCT, THE IPHONE.

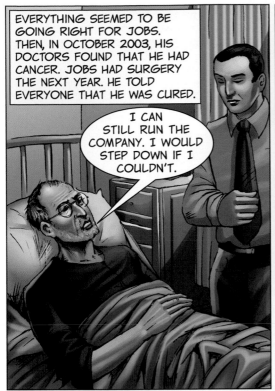

THE IPHONE COULD BE USED AS A PHONE AND AN IPOD. IT COULD CONNECT TO THE INTERNET. IT USED TOUCH-SCREEN TECHNOLOGY.

THERE WAS NOTHING ELSE LIKE IT. APPLE COMPUTERS HAD COME A LONG WAY FROM THE COMPANY JOBS HAD STARTED. IT NOW MADE MANY DIFFERENT TYPES OF PRODUCTS.

WE ARE DROPPING THE WORD "COMPUTERS" FROM OUR NAME AND CHANGING IT TO APPLE INC.

IN 2008, PEOPLE BEGAN TO WORRY ABOUT JOBS'S HEALTH. HE WAS VERY THIN AND DID NOT LOOK WELL. HE MISSED SOME IMPORTANT EVENTS.

I HAVE TO TELL THE REPORTERS WHY YOU WILL NOT BE AT THE NEXT APPLE EVENT.

TELL THEM I HAVE A COMMON BUG.

THE CANCER HAD SPREAD TO HIS LIVER. WITHOUT A **TRANSPLANT**, HE WOULD HAVE DIED.

JOBS WOULD NOT SAY THAT HIS CANCER HAD RETURNED. HOWEVER, HE TOOK SIX MONTHS OFF FROM WORK. IN APRIL 2009, HE HAD A LIVER TRANSPLANT.

JOBS WAS BACK AT APPLE TWO MONTHS LATER. HE WORKED AS HARD AS EVER. THERE WAS A NEW PRODUCT COMING OUT SOON, A TABLET COMPUTER.

I GUESS STEVE IS FEELING WELL AGAIN.

YES, HE IS TOUGHER ON US THAN BEFORE!

THE IPAD WAS INTRODUCED IN JANUARY 2010. APPLE FANS LINED UP TO BUY THEM.

IT LOOKS A LOT LIKE AN IPHONE.

I STARTED THE TABLET EARLIER BUT WANTED THE PHONE TO COME OUT FIRST.

A YEAR LATER, JOBS AGAIN TOOK TIME OFF FOR HEALTH REASONS. HE STILL WENT TO TRADE SHOWS TO ANNOUNCE NEW APPLE PRODUCTS. HOWEVER, HE LOOKED VERY THIN AND WEAK.

HIS CANCER MUST BE BACK.

HE LOOKS TOO WEAK TO STAND.

IN AUGUST 2011, JOBS STEPPED DOWN AS HEAD OF APPLE.

I ALWAYS SAID IF THERE CAME A DAY WHEN I COULD NO LONGER MEET MY DUTIES . . . I WOULD BE THE FIRST TO LET YOU KNOW.

UNFORTUNATELY, THAT DAY HAS COME.

AFTER STEVE LEFT APPLE, HE SPENT TIME WITH HIS FAMILY. HE HAD MARRIED LAURENE POWELL IN 1991, AND THE COUPLE HAD THREE CHILDREN.

ON OCTOBER 5, 2011, STEVE JOBS DIED. HE WAS 56. HIS FAMILY WAS WITH HIM. HIS LAST WORDS WERE, "OH WOW. OH WOW. OH WOW."

PEOPLE AROUND THE WORLD REACTED WITH GREAT SADNESS TO THE NEWS OF HIS DEATH. MORE THAN A MILLION PEOPLE WROTE SYMPATHY MESSAGES ON APPLE'S WEBSITE.

PEOPLE GATHERED AT APPLE STORES, AT APPLE HEADQUARTERS, AND AT HIS HOME TO **MOURN**.

BOTH JOBS'S FRIENDS AND **RIVALS** MOURNED HIS PASSING. THE LEADERS OF MANY COUNTRIES HONORED HIM, INCLUDING PRESIDENT OBAMA.

THERE MAY BE NO GREATER TRIBUTE TO STEVE'S SUCCESS THAN THE FACT THAT MUCH OF THE WORLD LEARNED OF HIS PASSING ON A DEVICE HE INVENTED.

JOBS INFLUENCED MUCH OF THE TECHNOLOGY THAT PEOPLE USE TODAY. HIS PRODUCTS SHOWED THAT A POWERFUL AND USEFUL TOOL COULD HAVE A SIMPLE AND BEAUTIFUL DESIGN.

STEVE JOBS'S PHILOSOPHY OF "THINK DIFFERENT" **INSPIRED** MILLIONS. HIS VISION CHANGED THE WAY PEOPLE USE TECHNOLOGY AND THE WAY THEY THINK ABOUT IT. HE CHANGED THE WAY PEOPLE LIVE.

Timeline

1955 Steven Paul Jobs is born to Joanne Schieble. His biological father is Abdulfattah Jandali. Paul and Clara Jobs are his adoptive parents.

1969 Steve meets Steve Wozniak.

1976 Jobs and Wozniak start Apple Computers. They assemble and try to sell Apple I computers.

1978 The Apple II is produced. It is one of the first personal computers on the market.

1981 IBM creates its own personal computer. It is Apple's biggest rival.

1984 Apple creates the Macintosh.

1985 Jobs loses control of Apple. He leaves the company and starts NeXT.

1986 Jobs buys Pixar for its computer animation technology.

1991 Steve marries Laurene Powell. They have a son later in the year.

1995 Pixar makes *Toy Story*. Its success helps Jobs come back after failures with NeXT.

1997 Jobs becomes head of Apple again.

1998 The iMac is introduced.

2001 The iPod is released. It is one of Apple's most successful products.

2003 Apple starts iTunes, an online music store. Later in the year, Jobs finds out he has cancer.

2007 Jobs introduces the iPhone. Apple Computers changes its name to Apple Inc.

2009 Jobs has a liver transplant.

2010 Apple releases the iPad.

2011 Jobs resigns as head of Apple. Two months later, he dies at the age of 56.

Glossary

adopted (uh-DOPT-ed) Raised a child who has other biological parents.

animation (a-nuh-MAY-shun) A way of making a movie by developing and using a series of drawings or computer graphics to create a sense of movement.

biological (by-uh-LAH-jih-kul) Related through birth.

bribed (BRYBD) Gave money or a favor in return for something else.

circuit board (SER-ket BORD) A board that has many electrical circuits and is used in a computer or other piece of electronic equipment.

devices (dih-VYS-ez) Objects, machines, or pieces of equipment that are made for a special purpose.

digital (DIH-juh-tul) A form of words, pictures, and sound that is readable by a computer.

electronic (ih-lek-TRAH-nik) Having to do with electricity and computers.

entrepreneur (on-truh-pruh-NUR) A businessperson who has started his or her own business.

graphics (GRA-fiks) Pictures, shapes, or words that are used in books, magazines, and in computer programs or games.

inspired (in-SPY-urd) Moved someone to do something.

mourn (MORN) To show or feel sadness.

network (NET-wurk) A system of computers and other equipment, such as printers, that are connected to each other.

personal computers (PERS-nul kum-PYOO-terz) Small computers designed to be used by people at home or in the office.

products (PRAH-dukts) Things that are produced.

professional (pruh-FESH-nul) Someone who is paid for what he or she does.

program (PROH-gram) To develop a set of instructions that tells a computer what to do.

rivals (RY-vulz) People who try to beat someone else at something.

software (SOFT-wayr) Computer files that are made to do certain tasks.

technology (tek-NAH-luh-jee) Advanced tools that help people do and make things.

transplant (TRANZ-plant) To move something, including an organ or tissue, from one place or individual to another.

visionary (VIH-zhuh-ner-ee) A person who dreams.

Index

Websites

Due to the changing nature of Internet links, PowerKids Press has developed an online list of websites related to the subject of this book. This site is updated regularly. Please use this link to access the list:

www.powerkidslinks.com/jgai/jobs/